The Weight of All the Rain

Abby Israels

BookLeaf
Publishing

India | USA | UK

Dedication

For the girls who were always one step ahead.

Acknowledgement

Thank you to every sleepless night, when my mind refused to rest and sketched out beautiful, impossible thoughts.

Thank you to my family, my best friends, and everyone else in my life who consistently listens to those thoughts and has inspired me to write them down.

Preface

This collection, born from a certain ache of the soul, is a map of varying feelings - ones that are fleeting and ones that tend to linger—

In these 21 poems, I've captured pieces of myself at times where I felt I was being shattered, reshaped, and ultimately grounded in new understandings. Each poem is a step along this winding path of healing, confronting one's raw edges, and piecing a new version of my own personal human existence together.

I invite you to join me in these pages and find remnants your own journey. Whether you've known heartbreak, joy, or the quiet hum of self-realization, I hope you feel seen, heard, and understood. This book is a shared heartbeat for anyone who's felt both the longing for and liberation of deep inward reflection.

It Was Like Looking In A Mirror

Looking at you
Was like looking right back at me—
A unique connection,
A rare commodity,
Standing there in front of me.

Bright lights blaring,
The chatter of hundreds fading,
All grew faint,
Silent,
When I was with you.

Cut from the same cloth,
You and me—
Slightly different shades
Of the same golden hue.

Comfortable enough
To admit the things
I'd never say to others,
Knowing you felt them too,

The same thoughts circling.

I'll never know why or how it came to be,
But it was real—
I know it was.
You felt it too.

The mirror you held before me,
Reflected truths I needed to see.
For that, I thank the universe,
For opening my eyes—
For bringing me you.

Where Will It Go?

Anything that has ever existed, will always
exist.
Even the space between all of us,
Where silent energy once flowed.
Particles borns from somewhere else,
Will shift, transform, and carry on.

What we have, for brief moments of time,
Will remain forever, woven into the fabric of
something eternal.
It doesn't vanish, because it can't possibly
dissolve—
There's comfort in knowing
What we were, will always evolve.

What You Couldn't Hold

Fleeting touches, promises left behind,
Glances from afar, always wondering where
you hide.

You thought you looked right through me,
But it was I who held the razor stare.
I chose to ignore what I could see—
I knew who you were, I was aware.

My love is powerful, a force to feel,
You should have known just how lucky—
All the comfort I could heal.
But you couldn't hold it, not for long,
Chasing ghosts while I played along.

Now your hands cling to a fading past,
While I've let go—free at last.

Words To Live By

Caring is no shame,
Open hearts and honest souls,
Love without hiding.

Small

In a man's frame, a small boy resides,
With dreams like paper boats on turbulent tides.
He struts through the world with bravado and noise,
Yet inside, he's still just a scared little boy.

His laughter is brittle, a mask he adorns,
Chasing validation, a king made of thorns.
Selfish in moments, he clings to his toys,
Oblivious to the chaos, the hurt he deploys.

He hides in the shadows, afraid of the light,
A prisoner of comfort, too weak for the fight.
The boy wears a smile, but it's all just a game,
A façade of confidence, hiding his shame.

Free To Be, You And Me

I found a book I adored as a child,
One that always made me feel something.
Opening its pages, nostalgia crept in,
And tears began to stain each line.

The book recognized the chemistry of the
water droplets,
Familiar with the tears that fell at eight,
Now greeted by the same tears at
twenty-six—
Yet, they carried something new.

These tears were wiser, heavier with history,
Laced with more pain, sorrow, and loss.
A bitter saltiness that wasn't there before,
Tears no longer innocent, but knowing.

Yet the book felt more than pain—
These tears, rich with memories,
Had seen more corners of the world,
Felt roaring laughter and boundless love.

Older, yes, but still spirited,

Still holding that glimmer of youth.
And as I read, the book smiled back,
An old friend, reminiscing alongside me.

I Bet You'll Think About Me

I'm sure you will still think of me,
When silence creeps in, something unseen.
You say you're fine, that you've moved on,
But my shadow lingers long after I'm gone.

You will see me in songs and movies we both
love, in people on the street.
In the spaces between where your thoughts
tend to stray.
You'll laugh with your friends, but you know
deep inside,
I haunt every corner of the other life you
denied.

Go ahead, try to forget, but you won't get
far—
A ghost in your mirror, the crack in your
heart.
You broke it, but darling, I'll never be
through,

Because I bet you think of me more than you'd ever admit to.

The Happy Girl And The Sad Boy

In a sunlit room, with flowers to show,
There was a happy girl, with a radiant glow.
Embarrassed about her loud laugh, that rang
so clear,
She offered a warmth, something that many
held dear.

In front of her, stood a boy, cloaked in sighs,
With eyes that held stories of previous
heartache and goodbyes.
He watched her, with his heart heavy, still,
Wondering if true joy was a thing he could
feel.

"Why do you smile?" he asked, voice low as
the night,
"When the world is so rough, and dreams fade
from sight?"

She paused for a moment, her laughter a
thread,
"Because I believe in the light that we have
the ability to spread.
Life's tales are vivid; they can break and they
can heal,
Your sorrow is valid; it's part of the song,
But together, my friend, we can find where
we belong."

So she reached for his hand, pulling him near,
Inviting him to soften and hear.
In their quiet connection, the gap started to
close,
The happy girl and the sad boy--two hearts
that chose.
For in each other's presence, they began to
see,
That joy and heartache can coexist,
beautifully free.

Saving Your Seat

I worry that I will always save you a seat in
the theatre, right next to me.
Just in case you decide you want to come and
finish the movie.

Am I Sick?

Cradling myself,
Sipping comfort in liquid disguise,
Why does this ache settle so deep?
I feel unwell.

Knowing that I will be cursed to remember
you
Far longer than I ever had you near.
Writing these gentle words about you,
While your cowardice swiftly whispered
What I had already feared,
Am I sick?

You called me a beacon of light,
Said my love brought you warmth
Yet you turned your gaze backward,
Chasing ghosts through familiar tears.

No, I am not the one who is sick—
Clinging to old problems, lingering in the
past
While I wrestle with truth you refused to see.

Last Seat At The Table

I watched them rise, one by one,
From the table we used to share.
Time stretched between us, a quiet pull,
Yet the memories still linger there.

Friends who once filled every corner,
Now chasing dreams in far-off lands,
Their laughter, though distant, still echoes
bright,
Like stars I can hold in my hands.

Brothers who grew beside me close,
Now carving paths of their own,
But the roots we share are steady and strong,
No matter how far we've grown.

And though new faces fill the chairs,
Where old ones used to be,
There's warmth in the way life circles around,
Bringing new stories to me.

I sit at the edge, the last to remain,
A witness to all that's been,

Each change a chapter, each loss a gain,
In the constant flow we live within.

The table may shift, but it never fades—
It grows, it says goodbye, it welcomes, it stays.

My Boss Knows Best

"You want the truth? About all of this?"
"I'm listening," you reply with a sigh.

"Heartbreak is an exquisite thing,
A rush of feeling in a world so dull—
It's a gift, really,
When most days pass by like a gust of wind."

"I guess," you say, voice low,
"But why does it have to cut so deep?
A sharp knife, twisting, cold."

"Here's the thing...
You already know what will be said.
His words, hollow, deeply unoriginal.
Sad, stupid, predictable.
He'll never change,
Trapped in his own endless cycle,
Cursed to live like this.

But you, you are fortunate.
You will be more—so much more.
You are so much more.

And I hope one day
You'll find peace in that."

You Ruined One Of My Favourite Songs

After a long day,
I glance at the passenger seat,
Tired.
But you're there,
We're there—sharing space,
A quiet comfort.

You grab my phone,
Play a song you've been eager to share.
You didn't know,
It was already one of my favourites.
I tried to hide the look on my face,
But I'm sure you saw—
Everyone saw.
Subtlety never came easy to me.

You played that song again,
And again.
Every time we were together,
We sang at the top of our lungs—
One of the best feelings.

But summer faded
Into the rustle of fallen leaves.
Now, I can't listen without mourning
What might have been.
The joy stolen,
The melody tainted by loss.

I've locked the song away,
Alongside the roller coaster summer,
Boxed with memories too fragile to touch.
I'm angry.
You ruined one of my favorite songs.

You're Late

We've been waiting for you,
You're late.
All eyes are fixated,
Don't close the gate.

You were given something that none of us
were,
Use it.
A thorn and her roses.
Intrepid daydreamer.
Starry-eyed hopeless romantic.

Let's dream of impossible things together.
That's what you've always known.
Don't leave us hanging,
The world desperately needs to be shown.

We will all paint your flowers for you.
Just lead us in the right direction.
You see our faces, you are home.
Red Queen, who needs to be reminded of her
reflection.

Hands That Catch The Fall

It was your best friends, awake till dawn,
Crying beside you, piecing together the
shattered months,
Sending voice notes like lifelines,
Checking in, holding space, making sure you
felt seen.

It was your siblings,
Proud of your strength, sharing their own
heartbreak scars,
Desperate to lighten the burden,
To take even a fragment of the weight from
your heart.

It was your mom, cooking your favourite
meal,
Your dad, distracting you with terrible jokes,
Trying to pull you back from the edge of your
sorrow.

It was the quiet reminders surrounding you—

How full your life truly is, how cherished you are,
How lucky you are to be loved this deeply.

And most of all, it was looking in the mirror,
Seeing someone who has learned, who knows better,
A woman ready to give her boundless heart
To people who will treasure it,
Rather than toss it away.

This is what love is.

You'll Never Be Happy

Always looking past what's in front of you,
Glancing over your shoulder, seeking
something new.
Blind to what's here, never stopping to see—
Lost in distractions, and never in me.

You want me waiting, just around the corner,
To fill the space when you need it warmer.
But never on my terms, never all in,
Holding back, letting nothing begin.

Turns out, you were just a side role,
A supporting act without control,
Meant to bask in borrowed light from me,
And fade when I stepped out of sight, you see.

I pity you, truly—
You'll never know what it means to feel fully.
To know yourself, to know what's right,
To love with intention, not out of fright.

My gut tells me, you'll always chase,

An endless search, an empty space.
Because the grass isn't greener, not in that
way—
Maybe you'll wake up, but not today.

Anchor

I always had it in me,
She always had it in her.
We've spent more hours talking and working
through storms
Than I have with anyone else.

She is wise, and so am I,
A mirror of truths and quiet reflection.
We offer different perspectives, different
voices—
A kaleidoscope of thought, never a moment
wasted.

Sleep is lost, yet energy stays high,
No one knows how we do it, how we get by.
It's a gift, we say, and sometimes a curse,
But we carry it all, for better or worse.

In the cold, we remain fierce.
A thread binding us, steadfast and long.
Together we lay, unshaken by time,
Our spirits enduring, weathering every
wrong.

She is my anchor, and I am hers,
I hear her voice, soft yet strong.
And I know, as night gives way to dawn,
We will always have it in us...we have all
along.

Shrinking Violet

Exposed chest wound.
Lying on my bed, feeling the trust pour out of
my body like a pool of blood.
Sheets are now stained with every fibre of
who I am.

What used to stand tall and proud,
Has sunken in, 6 feet under ground.

My mom has always told me,
"You are no shrinking violet".
It doesn't feel like that today.
I haven't felt like this in a long time.
How sad.

Re-writing

A plan waits, unshown,
standing at greatness's edge—
trust me, take my hand.

Mrs. Darling

As I grow older, I find my own way,
No longer yearning to be Wendy or Peter,
But to embody Mrs. Darling—
A spirit of grace, a heart that won't sway.

She holds a hidden kiss, profound and rare,
The kiss of maturity combined with eternal
youth,
A delicate balance, a secret affair,
Where wisdom dances with joy in its truth.

This kiss, a treasure, that cannot be given
away,
It is for me alone to make sure it stays.

For that kiss is integral, a part of my core,
A whisper of who I am meant to be,
A guiding light in the depths of my lore,
A testament to the dreams that run wild and
free.

It Rained When I Needed It To

I asked for the rain and I was brought a
storm.
I needed to feel the full extent of pain,
To be able to appreciate happiness.

Fighting off a flesh-eating disease to remind
myself
What my strength is capable of.
What my mind is capable of.

I feared drowning, but it makes you feel alive.
It makes you focus on your beating heart.
On the air inside of your lungs.
So, let it pour.